The Peacemaker's Wife

A journal for reflection & encouragement
for your life as a police wife

Rebecca Lynn

ISBN: 9781793390653
ISBN-13: 9781793390653

DEDICATION

Dedicated to my supportive husband. You are my backbone and motivation. I love you so very much. Thank you for your patience and encouragement daily.

And to my fellow police wives who walk along this journey with me.

CONTENTS

INTRODUCTION

Blessed are the peacemakers, for they shall be called the children of God.
-Matthew 5:9

As a peacemaker's wife, mother, former teacher, and natural people-pleaser, I have spent years, YEARS, doing for others and not investing in myself. Hardly any self-care, little reflection, and it began to wear on me.

It got to a point where, after our third child was born, I had no idea who I was anymore without the titles "mom," "police wife," etc. I felt rather lost even though those "titles" made me extremely happy every day.

That is until I took a leap of faith and flew to Jackson Hole, WY with many other women in my shoes, although I didn't know they were at the time. I spent 5 days pouring back into myself, as odd as it felt at first, with the amazing Chris Kyle Frog Foundation.

Matthew 5:9, WEB

My eyes finally opened to the lack of mental care I was giving myself as I stretched on a yoga mat early one morning. I was in a room full of other first responder and military wives, but yet, I was so in tune with myself. Yoga? When in the world was the last time I did yoga? When had I even slowed down? When was the last time I thought about what I needed?

The fact of the matter was, I was running from sun up til sun down, never reflecting about my day, never thinking about what I wanted. I realized on that yoga mat that slowing down felt good. I no longer wanted to live in a hamster wheel. I wanted to be more in tune with my emotions and know that each day I was doing my best and my best was good enough.

I left that trip feeling re-energized, focused on my personal goals and at peace. And now, I've made a promise to myself to maintain that, and it is my passion to help you & fellow police wives do the same.

Our spouses strive to bring the highest level of peace into the world day after day without question. No matter the level of cruelty, hurt, danger, or negativity they encounter, they continue their quest for peace. As a peacemaker's wife, we continue that same goal ourselves and within our homes. We work tirelessly to seek perfection, even when perfection is not needed, nor does it exist. We often carry the weight at home, feeling on duty ourselves, without much reprieve. But too often, our role as a peacemaker's wife, allows us to forget the importance of pouring back into ourselves, even when we need it most.

Whether you take 5 minutes a day or five hours a week, you deserve to keep YOU at center focus. Whether you need to refocus after a hard day or you need to remember that you are enough, I hope this journal provides that for you. I hope you give to yourself each and every day because you are so worth it.

My hope is that this journal will encourage you to:

Remember : think back, recall memories, put you on the right foot for the day and allow you to recognize good days rather than bad.

Refuel: fill up your heart, mind and soul with encouragement and positive thinking.

Re-energize: pour back into yourself by saying "no" more to outside influences, saying "yes" to yourself more often, clear out negativity and reward yourself.

Restore: make positive growth or changes in areas like: marriage, self-care, friendships, faith, life goals, etc.

Refocus: change a bad mood, see the positive and/or change your perspective.

Author Recommendations:

Some days you may open this journal and begin where you left off, reflecting one day at a time. Other days you may be searching for guidance or encouragement based on how you are feeling right now. Use this index to look up journal pages for what you need today or tomorrow.

For when you are:

Needing motivation, turn to pages: 17, 25, 45, 96

Building self-confidence, turn to pages: 88, 90, 92, 103

Lonely (or missing your spouse), turn to pages: 30, 46, 48, 58, 64, 76, 114

Fearful, worrisome or sad, turn to pages: 37, 40, 52, 89

Needing friendship, turn to pages: 21, 26, 59, 62

Tired or overwhelmed, turn to pages: 20, 28, 32, 33, 74, 77, 80, 102

A note from the author

To my fellow blue sister,

I write this journal for you because I see your need to refuel, re-energize and pour back into your soul. I want you to make the most of your life as a police wife without feeling like you have to stress in the process. It is important that you remember your "job" as a police wife needs to not consume you. It is a part of you, but it is not the only you.

My goal with this journal is that you take time when you need it most to re-energize, refocus, remember, and restore areas of your life. Whether that time is at night before you sleep, when you are fresh in the morning and drinking your coffee, or when your officer has worked many days and hours and you are at your limit. Whether you open this book daily or when you are desperately seeking motivation and peace or a place to vent. Let this be your safe place. Your own diary of thoughts, prayers and reflection.

While we walk similar shoes, our journeys are uniquely different. Your journey is truly your own, so be confident in that. Own it and know, police wife, you are amazing.

Love,
Rebecca

Some days you will think you can't handle anything more, but only in hindsight do you see just how strong you are.

Remember

Your life as a police wife (or girlfriend) may just be starting out or you may feel that you are knee-deep into this life. Either way, think about how it started for you. Were you (are you) a girlfriend? How did you feel? How have you changed over time?

_____

_____

_____

_____

_____

_____

_____

_____

_____

_____

_____

Restore

It is time to look deep within. Look past the surface. What do you love most about yourself?

_____

_____

_____

_____

_____

_____

_____

_____

_____

_____

_____

_____

_____

_____

Be the police wife YOU want to be, not who you *think* you should be.

Re-energize

Stop worrying about what MORE you can do in life or what MORE you can do for your officer. Always having the mentality that you have to do MORE without stopping to give yourself credit for your accomplishments will run you dry. It will burst your bubble and you will always be in a hamster wheel of self-doubt. It is time to start thinking about what you *actually* do. It is time to give yourself credit. Write down ANY small or large accomplishments from this week for the season of life YOU are in. Don't ever worry about how others will view YOUR accomplishments.

_____

_____

_____

_____

_____

_____

_____

_____

Remember

True or False. This lifestyle overwhelms me, but it is worth it to me.

_____

_____

_____

_____

_____

_____

_____

_____

_____

_____

_____

_____

_____

Restore

Think about your #tribe.

Who are the people who help you the most? Encourage you, believe in you, are nonjudgemental. List them here and keep this circle close. Refer back to these amazing people when negativity strikes in your life or you need someone to confide in or lean on.

_____

_____

_____

_____

_____

_____

_____

_____

_____

_____

Re-energize

Sometimes we feel the need to do all the things. We do this until we realize, we are exhausted and have nothing left to give. When is the last time you said "no"? What can you start saying "no" to (big or small) to help you make the most of your life as a police wife?

Just saying "no" to staying late at work or cooking a full blown, healthy dinner can feel liberating. Or maybe you say you can't attend one more event this month because your plate is full. Or doing all the housework by yourself just can't happen this week- just commit to what you feel is reasonable for the time being. You can do this!

_____

_____

_____

_____

_____

_____

_____

It always seems unreachable until you do it yourself, again and again.

Refuel

If you could send one positive message to your future
police wife self, what would it be?

_____

_____

_____

_____

_____

_____

_____

_____

_____

_____

_____

_____

_____

_____

Remember

When is the last time you have asked for help?

I'm not talking about the kind of help you need if you get locked out of the house. I am talking about realizing you can not solve every problem or that it is okay to be tired.

Have you asked someone to watch your kids, if you have them, so you can go grocery shopping alone? Have you asked your spouse to help you with errands or housework because you are having a stressful or busy week? Have you asked your mother-in-law (gulp) to take over planning the family party because you can't realistically get it done?

I'll ask again. When is the last time you have asked for help? How can asking for help, help you?

_____

_____

_____

_____

_____

Re-energize

A police wife can take on many roles which leads to exhaustion and overwhelm. Name three things that just aren't working for you. Which of those can you vow to change for next week and the weeks to come?

For example, maybe you are rushing every morning, so packing your officer's meals is something you have to stop doing. Or maybe waking up 30 minutes earlier each day to work out or write in this journal would help you so you can start your day off on the right foot.

_____

_____

_____

_____

_____

_____

_____

_____

You married a person, not just an officer. There is more to your officer just like there is more to you.

Refuel

What makes you feel great about yourself?
Doing your hair each day? Compliments? A good start to
your morning? Eating healthy? List them below.

_____

_____

_____

_____

_____

_____

_____

_____

_____

_____

_____

_____

Restore

Sometimes even the roughest of days can bring laughter, love and happiness. What is something that made you laugh this week?

_____

_____

_____

_____

_____

_____

_____

_____

_____

_____

_____

_____

Re-energize

List 5 things that help you relax. What is one that you can easily commit to do today?

_____

_____

_____

_____

_____

_____

_____

_____

_____

_____

_____

_____

_____

Refuel

We all need encouragement to get through the hardest of days. Whether it is a small pick me up for your officer or taking dinner to a friend that has helped you recently or calling someone when you feel they may need uplifting words. Who is someone you could help or encourage this week? What could you do for them?

_____

_____

_____

_____

_____

_____

_____

_____

_____

_____

_____

_____

Pour into others, not just yourself. But be sure to pour into yourself first.

Refocus

When stress arises because of police wife life, what plan(s) do you have in place to help you keep control?

_____

_____

_____

_____

_____

_____

_____

_____

_____

_____

_____

_____

_____

Refuel

You are strong. You are resilient. You do things well, and you do them uniquely. Name two things you do well and make you proud.

_____

_____

_____

_____

_____

_____

_____

_____

_____

_____

_____

_____

Refocus

Let's talk about grace. It is so important to not only give yourself grace but extend it to those around you. We don't know how our day will be laid out, or what our officer will encounter on shift making each day special and unique. But it can also feel scary, worrisome, or like we are losing control. Today I want you to extend someone GRACE. This someone could be you, your officer or anyone else in your life that may need it.

_____

_____

_____

_____

_____

_____

_____

_____

Don't let the fear of what you CAN'T control, control you.

Refocus

I want you to focus today on what you have, not what could be or what is missing. Don't size up your life to a friend, coworker, or your ideal life five years from now. What is ONE thing you have today that makes your life special and amazing?

_____

_____

_____

_____

_____

_____

_____

_____

_____

_____

_____

_____

Restore

Who are YOU?

I am

_____

_____

_____

I am

_____

_____

_____

I am

_____

_____

_____

Refuel

To navigate this lifestyle well, you must allow yourself to give permission. Permission to eat cereal for dinner. Permission to not be organized. Permission to be tired and not do it all. Today is that day. What are you giving yourself permission to do or not do?

_____

_____

_____

_____

_____

_____

_____

_____

_____

_____

_____

_____

When your strength is tested,
your endurance will grow.

Remember

Success. We want each day to lead to a path of success but sometimes we only measure success by the largest wins we see. What are your small, even teeny tiny successes for today?

_____

_____

_____

_____

_____

_____

_____

_____

_____

_____

_____

Restore

Feeling connected to your officer can be a constant battle. We long for closeness but that closeness is not always ideal after tiring shifts and time apart. Consider taking a love language test to see how you can connect with your spouse more.

If you already know your love languages, what are you doing to say "I love you" in your spouse's language? Or how is your spouse saying "I love you" to you? Write them down or reflect on them to bring closeness to your relationship.

_____

_____

_____

_____

_____

_____

Refocus

Extend grace for your officer on days nothing is done around your house or he/she may be grumpy from many long hours at work. When you are compelled to feel angry or frustrated today over small things, extend grace.

_____

_____

_____

_____

_____

_____

_____

_____

_____

_____

_____

Remember

Your journey is yours. It is unlike anyone else's. Your foundation is different. Your walls are different. And your story can only be told by you. Take time to write down part of your story today. Maybe it is your love story. Maybe it is your story of self-care, similar to mine in the introduction. Or maybe you want to reflect on your story as a peacemaker's wife.

_____

_____

_____

_____

_____

_____

_____

_____

_____

_____

Refuel

Sometimes we are our own worst critics. We see what we should be doing more of, what we aren't good at, and how other people seem to do everything better and more successfully. The idea of perfectionism is rooted in evil and can lead us down a dark mindset if we let it control us. Instead, embrace imperfections. Be happy with who you are and what you accomplish each and every day. Lead yourself on a path of brilliant self-confidence. What are your best imperfections?

_____

_____

_____

_____

_____

_____

_____

_____

_____

Re-energize

Equip yourself with the right tools for success. Know that what you are doing right now is enough and invest in yourself and the law enforcement lifestyle to have more tools for later on in your journey. What tools do you need more of right now? What would it take to attain those tools?

Maybe you need resources for successfully navigating police wife life. Maybe you need to hear positive stories of others in your shoes. Reflect on what tools you need most.

_____

_____

_____

_____

_____

_____

_____

_____

Remember

If this lifestyle has taught us anything, it is to never take anything for granted. What do you truly appreciate?

_____

_____

_____

_____

_____

_____

_____

_____

_____

_____

_____

_____

_____

Restore

Burnout. It gets us all, am I right? Long days, lonely nights, doing it all when we have no other choice. At some point our body tells us to take a break. What does "a break" mean for you? Whether you need a break now or next week, what do you dream of a break to be?

Sometimes a pedicure or long run is what you need but even the simplest of ideas can recharge us, like sipping hot coffee alone in the wee hours of morning.

_____

_____

_____

_____

_____

_____

_____

_____

Look at you!

You. are. rocking it!

Restore

The thin blue line. The line that we all hold so sacred. But often it can feel like our officer's stand on one side as we stand on the other. How can you and your officer work as a team this week, hand in hand on the same blue line?

Maybe this means putting aside arguments for one week, giving one another more grace, or picking up slack even though you are tired. Meet each other in the middle this week with the objective that you will walk this journey together.

_____

_____

_____

_____

_____

_____

_____

_____

Refocus

Often when we feel alone we think it is a reflection on us, that maybe we are doing something wrong. When in reality, it could very well be a blessing that we just can't see yet. Maybe we need that alone time to think, reflect or grow fonder of a spouse we miss. What is something you can do or think about the next time you are alone?

_____

_____

_____

_____

_____

_____

_____

_____

_____

_____

Refuel

Strength. A word that feels so strong but yet is subjective. Sometimes we look stronger on the outside than we are on the inside. But no matter our weaknesses, we all possess strength. In what ways do you feel strong?

_____

_____

_____

_____

_____

_____

_____

_____

_____

_____

_____

Re-energize

The sky's the limit. We are only limited by ourselves. What do you want to reach high for today?

_____

_____

_____

_____

_____

_____

_____

_____

_____

_____

_____

_____

_____

_____

Re-energize

As a peacemaker's wife, we may put walls up and not easily allow others to enter. We may have a hard time trusting. This may happen with new friendships, but it could just as easily happen with old ones, too. What walls can you break down today to allow yourself to receive help or let others in? Or just be open minded today to allow people in just a bit more than you did yesterday.

Remember

Our love for our officer is what brought us into this lifestyle. What is the best memory you have of you and your officer **because** of the job?

_____

_____

_____

_____

_____

_____

_____

_____

_____

_____

_____

_____

Restore

Making and fostering friendships often goes low on the totem pole as a peacemaker's wife. It can feel difficult to find others who truly relate to us. Decide what type of setting for meeting and fostering relationships works best for your life: meeting fellow police wives online, attending a local moms group, going out with co-workers after work. Pencil one in this week and make time for a friendship: new or old.

Refuel

Comparison. It's human nature to compare. We compare ourselves, relationships, careers, materialistic items. But comparison can put us further back instead of moving forward, if we let it. Instead, be comfortable in your own skin and only compare your today to your yesterday. What's one thing you are doing better today than yesterday?

_____

_____

_____

_____

_____

_____

_____

_____

_____

_____

Refocus

When our situations feel hard, too tough to handle, or maybe scary, we wait for the future to be different and hope the future will start relatively soon. Instead, of waiting, today is the day to do something about it. Start your future today by taking one step forward. Maybe you are in an unwanted job or have financial issues that seem too large to tackle. Whatever the case may be, move forward on that journey today, instead of hoping for change.

_____

_____

_____

_____

_____

_____

_____

_____

_____

Start today. Move forward. Be YOUR change.

Refocus

How are you physically feeling today? Tired, well-rested, hungry, hurting? Give yourself ten minutes today, longer if you need to, to soothe those physical feelings with maybe a walk, stretches or hot bath. What will help you most today?

_____

_____

_____

_____

_____

_____

_____

_____

_____

_____

_____

_____

Remember

What is one thing you must do every day to ensure you have a successful day? Do you ever forget or run out of time? How do you feel when that happens?

_____

_____

_____

_____

_____

_____

_____

_____

_____

_____

_____

_____

_____

Forget perfection.

Be imperfect.

Ditch all the notions that you *should* be someone you are not.

Refuel

Flexibility will strengthen me. How can you be flexible today?

_____

_____

_____

_____

_____

_____

_____

_____

_____

_____

_____

_____

Give grace.

Refocus

The role of a peacemaker's wife can often require so much of us. It feels as if we are the only one bending, twisting or giving in this lifestyle. But this flexibility will only make you stronger and allow you to grow as a person. Why is flexibility a strength of yours? (Any example counts, even a small one).

_____

_____

_____

_____

_____

_____

_____

_____

_____

_____

_____

_____

Loneliness will NOT control me.

Remember

You may not see it now, but each day you are preparing yourself to be a stronger version of yourself. Think of how much stronger you are today than you were last year. Two years ago. Five years ago. How do you see yourself as stronger than the past?

_____

_____

_____

_____

_____

_____

_____

_____

_____

_____

_____

A little time together is better than NO time.

Refocus

What are the little things in life that help you feel
motivated or empowered? Influential music, a latte or a ten
minute walk? Think of what helps you the most but doesn't
require a ton of work or money. Doing these little things
can reset you on your journey as a peacemaker's wife.

_____

_____

_____

_____

_____

_____

_____

_____

_____

_____

_____

_____

Refuel

Saying yes to everything all the time won't make you the best police wife, mother, friend. It will make you a tired person with no boundaries. What do you HAVE to say yes to today? What can wait until tomorrow?

_____

_____

_____

_____

_____

_____

_____

_____

_____

_____

_____

_____

Re-energize

Today is about taking everything in and slowing down.
What do you notice about how you are feeling today? Take
time to listen, watch, and give yourself permission to not
fall victim to hustle and bustle.

_____

_____

_____

_____

_____

_____

_____

_____

_____

_____

_____

_____

_____

Just show up. That's all you have to do today. Show up.

Re-energize

What is one word, phrase or mantra you can keep in the front of your mind today that will help you?

_____

_____

_____

_____

_____

_____

_____

_____

_____

_____

_____

_____

_____

_____

Refuel

Name 5 things that make you smile. Try to encounter one of these things today.

_____

_____

_____

_____

_____

_____

_____

_____

_____

_____

_____

_____

_____

_____

Restore

High hopes. We all have them. We like to set goals, dream, think of the future. What are your goals, in any aspect of life, for the next month? 6 months? Year?

Keep these goals and refer to them often so you can always strive to make them happen.

_____

_____

_____

_____

_____

_____

_____

_____

_____

_____

_____

Re-energize

Are you a thinker? Doer? Maker? What word fits you the most? Do you make time in your schedule to think, do or make/create? If not, where can you fit time in your calendar to do something you love just for you?

_____

_____

_____

_____

_____

_____

_____

_____

_____

_____

_____

Refuel or Re-energize

What is one fear that is currently in your life? Fear seems to tie closely with our officer's job, but finding ways to minimize that fear is what matters. Identify this fear and think of one way you can minimize it today.

Maybe this means turning off social media, a scanner, talking to someone about your feelings. Get one step closer to kicking that fear to the curb by committing to one action today.

_____

_____

_____

_____

_____

_____

_____

_____

_____

You can totally do this. And you can do it well.

Re-energize

There's negativity all around us. At your officer's job, your work, the media. It will be there every day. But today will be different. Today you are going to fill your mind with positivity and drown out the negativity around you. Refuse to allow that negativity in. REFUSE IT, my friend.

Write down the first positive or powerful word that comes to your mind and carry it with you all day to help drown out the negative.

_____

_____

_____

_____

_____

_____

_____

_____

I'm not perfect and that is okay.

Remember

The struggle to find a true and perfect balance as a peacemaker's wife does not exist. Instead we can strive to find the best in every situation and know that what we are doing each and every day is enough. Stop searching.

_____

_____

_____

_____

_____

_____

_____

_____

_____

_____

_____

_____

You are worthy.

Restore

It's important to surround yourself with people who understand you, support you and challenge you. It's important to recognize those people in your life that are there for the right reasons. And it's okay to say goodbye to those who aren't. Who are the most uplifting people in your life? Make a promise to be around those positive people more often.

_____

_____

_____

_____

_____

_____

_____

_____

_____

_____

Refocus

What do you want to conquer or kick-butt at today?

_____

_____

_____

_____

_____

_____

_____

_____

_____

_____

_____

_____

_____

_____

Remember

What do you think about the most during the day (top 2)?
Do you wish they were different? Do these thoughts
sabotage, consume or control your day? Or are you happy
with these thoughts?

_____

_____

_____

_____

_____

_____

_____

_____

_____

_____

_____

_____

Refocus

Write as many aspects of your police wife life that you can think of that you LOVE.

Think about: What makes this lifestyle worth it? Have there been amazing people you have met along the way? Do you view the time you have or don't have with loved ones differently because of this lifestyle?

_____

_____

_____

_____

_____

_____

_____

_____

_____

_____

Refocus

Today I am…

Tomorrow I will be….

Reflect on how you are feeling emotionally today and if you need a shift of those emotions for tomorrow.

_____

_____

_____

_____

_____

_____

_____

_____

_____

_____

_____

Together, with you, is my favorite place to be.

Re-energize

Too often we forget to reward ourselves for the little (or even big) things we accomplish in our lives. Life gets too busy. We feel those accomplishments are things we *should* be doing in life. But we must take time to notice all that we do.

How can you reward yourself today for your accomplishments, big or small?

_____

_____

_____

_____

_____

_____

_____

_____

_____

_____

Refocus

Stop wishing. It's time to start doing. What is something that you can move higher on your priority list today?

_____

_____

_____

_____

_____

_____

_____

_____

_____

_____

_____

_____

Restore

What is your current mindset about your officer's career and its impact on your life? How does it make you feel?

Are you happy with those feelings? What would you change, if anything? Have you shared these thoughts with your spouse?

_____

_____

_____

_____

_____

_____

_____

_____

_____

_____

_____

_____

Re-energize

Take a deep breath and keep trying. Again and again. Today is about a fresh start and breathing your way through the day. Come back to this page at the end of your day.

What did breathing do for you today? Were you able to focus, think better, slow down? What did you notice?

_____

_____

_____

_____

_____

_____

_____

_____

_____

_____

_____

Remember

Remember that your journey is yours. Own and love your journey because it belongs to you. Be different and embrace the fact that you don't have to be like everyone else. Why is your journey special?

_____

_____

_____

_____

_____

_____

_____

_____

_____

_____

_____

_____

Restore

Don't get so wrapped up in being perfect and doing #allthethings that you let it steal your happiness. Instead, focus on the things that matter most. Focus on your priorities and let everything else go. You don't have to be a police wife that has meals cooked, a clean home and acts as both mom and dad many nights of the week. Maybe just pick one of those things that is a priority to your family that you can do well. Reflect on your priorities today and make sure you are at the top of that list.

_____

_____

_____

_____

_____

_____

_____

_____

Refuel

Sometimes we are so focused on doing more and being better, that we forget that what we are doing right now is good enough. What qualities do you possess RIGHT NOW that make you simply amazing?

_____

_____

_____

_____

_____

_____

_____

_____

_____

_____

_____

_____

_____

_____

Refuel

Take charge of your own greatness today. You have something to offer. You have the ability to do great things. Show that off today.

_____

_____

_____

_____

_____

_____

_____

_____

_____

_____

_____

_____

Refuel

Show up for YOURSELF today. How can YOU, and only YOU, be your biggest cheerleader today? Don't let anyone or anything bring you down.

_____

_____

_____

_____

_____

_____

_____

_____

_____

_____

_____

_____

_____

Be kind to yourself. You are even more amazing today than you were yesterday.

Restore

Don't worry today about people's opinions of you. You can't change them, so it's not worth your time trying. Just be a confident you. What steps can you take to make that happen?

_____

_____

_____

_____

_____

_____

_____

_____

_____

_____

_____

Refocus

We truly have the toughest jobs, saying goodbye to our loved one each and every day before they begin a shift. Then trying to stay a float, organized, and play every other role so well. Remember that all that matters is that you do your BEST. Your best is good enough.

_____

_____

_____

_____

_____

_____

_____

_____

_____

_____

_____

_____

Re-energize

What is the calm to your chaos? What relaxes you and have you taken time to embrace that calm today?

_____

_____

_____

_____

_____

_____

_____

_____

_____

_____

_____

_____

_____

_____

Refocus

If you are a peacemaker's wife that feels overwhelmed, tired and living in a mode of 24/7, please know that saying NO to your cup that is pouring over is okay, it is actually encouraged. What can bring your cup to below full today?

_____

_____

_____

_____

_____

_____

_____

_____

_____

_____

_____

_____

_____

_____

Remember

Why did you marry or start dating your spouse? Think about why you love him/her. Let go of the underwear on the floor, dirty dishes, or any little things that may upset you today. When you feel upset or annoyed, think of how your heart finally rests when you hear velcro and they are safe in your home after shift. Don't sweat the small stuff today.

_____

_____

_____

_____

_____

_____

_____

_____

_____

_____

Final Thoughts

I truly hope this journal brought you either daily encouragement or motivation and support during a time of need. The best advice I have to you as a fellow peacemaker's wife is to just keep doing the best you can. Your "best" does not mean perfect. It does not mean to make yourself tired doing too much or giving to others instead of yourself. Your best means that what you have to offer each day is going to be good enough. Good enough for yourself and for others.

You got this!

Acknowledgements

While I believe this journal is so needed for my fellow police wives, I also know this would not have been written if it were not for so many police wives cheering me on and giving me support. I am so very grateful for each and every one of you and I love that we are on this journey together. And a special shoutout to all my CKFF sisters and to my amazing friends, Cynthia, Aimee & Jamie- I love you all.

Also, a huge thank you to my husband for giving me the encouragement to get this journal to completion and for always giving me the time to work on my passion helping law enforcement families. I love you so very much.

And without a doubt, I have to thank my friend and editor, Erin. Erin, your knowledge and patience are outstanding. You guided me and gave me so many wonderful suggestions that my tired mind would have never thought of. As a fellow blue sister, you were the perfect one for the job.

About the Author

Rebecca is the founder of Proud Police Wife (.com), a blog dedicated to providing support and resources to police wives and their families. Every month her website reaches thousands nationally and brings encouragement to fellow law enforcement families. Rebecca is a police wife of 13 years, mother of three and former elementary education teacher.

Made in the USA
San Bernardino, CA
02 June 2019